THE *Bone* DETECTIVES

How Forensic Anthropologists Solve Crimes and Uncover Mysteries of the Dead

by Donna M. Jackson

Photographs by Charlie Fellenbaum

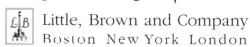
Megan Tingley Books

Little, Brown and Company
Boston New York London

To Charlie and Christopher Jackson, with love
— D. M. J.

To all my teachers and to Cindy
— C. F.

First Paperback Edition

Epigraph on page 4 from *Archaeological Perspectives on the Battle of Little Bighorn*,
by Douglas D. Scott, Richard A. Fox, Jr., Melissa A. Connor, and Dick Harmon.
Copyright © 1989 by the University of Oklahoma Press.
Reprinted by permission of the University of Oklahoma Press.

Newspaper clippings on page 33 courtesy of *St. Louis Post-Dispatch*

Skeleton diagram on page 48 from *Clinical Anatomy for Medical Students,* by Richard S. Snell.
Copyright © 1995 by Richard S. Snell, M.D., Ph.D.
Reprinted by permission of Little, Brown, and Company (Inc.).

Library of Congress Cataloging-in-Publication Data

Jackson, Donna.
    The bone detectives : how forensic anthropologists solve crimes
and uncover mysteries of the dead / by Donna M. Jackson ;
photographs by Charlie Fellenbaum. — 1st ed.
        p.   cm.
    Includes index.
    Summary: Explores the world of forensic anthropology and its
applications in solving crimes.
    ISBN 0-316-82935-8 (hc) / ISBN 0-316-82961-7 (pb)
    1. Forensic anthropology — Juvenile literature.   [1. Forensic
anthropology.   2. Forensic sciences.   3. Criminal investigation.]
I. Fellenbaum, Charlie, ill.   II. Title.
GN69.8.J33   1996
363.2'5 — dc20   95-19051

                    HC: 10 9 8 7 6 5 4
                    PB: 10 9 8 7 6 5 4 3 2 1

                                SC

                        Printed in Hong Kong

Previous page:
Dr. Michael Charney of the Forensic Science Laboratory in Fort Collins, Colorado, uses his bone-reading
skills to identify skulls and skeletons.

Acknowledgments

Thanks to all who offered their time and assistance in creating this book, especially: bone detective Dr. Michael Charney and forensic sculptor Nita Bitner; Sgt. Mark Olin and the staff at the Denver Police Department's Crime Laboratory; Lt. Armedia Gordin; Sgt. Bill Conway, Sgt. Don Bizelli, and the Missouri State Highway Patrol; St. Charles County prosecuting attorney Tim Braun and paralegal Marilyn Lamb; forensic sculptor Betty Pat Gatliff; Dr. Clyde Snow; Dr. Doug Scott at the National Park Service; Dr. Michael Finnegan at Kansas State University; Dr. Eric Meikle at the Institute of Human Origins; Dr. Doug Owsley at the Smithsonian Institution's National Museum of Natural History; Dr. Ann Marie Mires at the University of Massachusetts; Drs. Boris Kondratieff and Patrick Fitzhorn at Colorado State University; John Gurche and the Denver Museum of Natural History; Teena Orling; Ken Nimmich at the FBI's Forensic Science Research and Training Center; Dr. Robert Lorenz; Donna Joy Newman; the *Greeley Tribune;* and up-and-coming bone detective Hannah Fuhr.

Special thanks to Dr. Owsley for reviewing the manuscript; Charlie Fellenbaum for his spine-tingling photographs; Dana Coffield for suggesting I get in touch with her friend the children's book editor; Megan Shaw Tingley for believing in the book; and all the students who shared in this project and helped make it a joy to write. — D. M. J.

I'm grateful to many for their cooperation in helping me create and assemble the hundreds of images that were considered for *The Bone Detectives,* no less so to those who I photographed and don't find themselves in these pages. We just couldn't use them all!

A special thanks first to author Donna Jackson, who gave me the opportunity to be part of this fascinating project.

Also to: Dr. Michael Charney and Nita Bitner; Sgt. Don Bizelli; Kitty Deernose at the Little Bighorn Battlefield National Monument; Dr. Doug Owsley; Sgt. Mark Olin and Criminalist William McDougall; Dr. Boris Kondratieff; Gary Hubiak, D.D.S.; Sylvia Wyant, Carol Herrick, and Jane Schmid, who lent their children; to those who helped me grow as a photographer, especially Gary Rehn, Vern Walker, and Jerry Cleveland; and to the Eastman Kodak Company for their fine-grain Lumiere films and Photo Craft Laboratories of Boulder for their great slide processing. — C. F.

As those who study them have come to learn, bones make good witnesses — although they speak softly, they never lie and they never forget.

— Dr. Clyde Collins Snow, forensic anthropologist

Contents

The Bone Detectives

More than two hundred bones hold our bodies together, and each one tells a story.

Some reveal our height. Some divulge our race and sex. Some even share information about foods we've eaten, limbs we've broken, and diseases we've suffered.

Not every bone tattles freely, however. Some bones say more than others.

But they all tell their secrets to the few who speak their language: forensic anthropologists, such as Dr. Michael Charney of the Forensic Science Laboratory at Colorado State University.

Dr. Charney is a "bone detective" who uses his bone-reading skills to help police crack complex cases involving unidentified human remains.

Lining the walls of his office are the skulls and skeletons of people who have lost their lives to accidents, homicides, or time. Most of the specimens are designed to be used for teaching, but some boxes of bones remain nameless. They hold stories longing to be told, mysteries waiting to be solved.

That's Dr. Charney's job.

When all that's left is a skeleton, he studies the bones for subtle clues that will help identify the dead.

"We're a rare breed," says Dr. Charney, who is one of only about 175 bone detectives practicing in the United States and Canada. "We're trained to extract the most amount of information from the least amount of bone."

Most bone detectives earn doctorate degrees in physical anthropology and spend years studying human skulls and skeletons of ancient peoples. Many go on to teach and conduct research at universities and museums. Others work for military organizations.

The techniques physical anthropologists apply to determine the sex, race, age, and height of humankind's earliest skeletons are

Students in Dr. Charney's lab study skulls and learn how human bones fit together.

the same ones they use to help officials identify historical figures, war casualties, and victims of fires, floods, and plane crashes.

They're also the skills they use when collaborating with police and other forensic scientists to help solve criminal cases.

When homicide is suspected, identifying the victim often leads police to the assailant. It also allows the victim's family to grieve with finality — knowing what's become of their loved one.

Who died?

How?

Why?

When and where?

These are all questions forensic scientists seek to answer. The pathologist examines the body and its tissue; the forensic dentist studies teeth and analyzes bite marks; the fingerprint examiner classifies and compares prints; and the serologist studies blood and body fluids.

In most cases, these techniques are sufficient — especially when a body is found and there's enough physical evidence to identify victims and reconstruct crimes.

But what if there is no body to examine? No fingerprints to lift? No bloodstains to analyze?

What if all that remains is a skeleton?

Grave Beginnings

Forensic anthropology dates back about 145 years. One of the first cases involved a skeletal identification made by a forensics team led by Dr. Jeffries Wyman, a Harvard University anatomy professor, whom many call the father of forensic anthropology.

Wyman was recruited to work on a famous court case involving the death of a prominent Boston-area doctor named George Parkman. The accused murderer was a colleague of Parkman's named Dr. John White Webster, a well-known professor at Harvard Medical School. Webster owed Parkman money, and on November 23, 1849, Parkman went to claim it.

That was the last time anyone saw him alive.

Less than a week later, the janitor at the Medical School called the police with a grisly discovery. Hidden in a stone vault beneath Webster's office were what appeared to be human remains. Sure enough, when police arrived, they retrieved about 150 bones — some of them burned — and a set of false teeth. Officers suspected the bones belonged to Parkman but left it up to a team of doctors and dentists to prove it in court.

The doctors examined the remains and testified that they matched a person of Parkman's age, build, and height.

One of the most convincing witnesses turned out to be Parkman's dentist, who recognized the set of dentures he had designed for the victim. Parkman had a unique lower jaw and needed a special mold made for his false teeth. The dentist demonstrated how the dentures police found fit this unusual mold.

After only three hours of deliberation, the jury found Webster guilty of murder. The next day, the judge sentenced him to hang, which he did in August of 1850.

Dr. Jeffries Wyman led one of the first teams of scientists to use forensic anthropology, identifying skeletal remains to help solve a crime.

A skull lies hidden in the woods.

The Case of the Shining Skull

November 1987: A mapmaker from Finland spies a round object as he surveys the grounds of a Boy Scout camp near Farmington, Missouri. Believing he's spotted a large turtle shell, the man inches closer.

Suddenly he sees that the smooth, sunbleached object isn't a turtle shell. It's a human skull.

Confused and a bit frightened, the man waits nearly three months before reporting the discovery to his supervisor at the local orienteering club. Soon after, he returns home to Finland.

The supervisor searches the 5,400-acre Boy Scout ranch for the skull but fails to find it hidden among the hundreds of trees and fallen leaves. In March 1988, she returns to the remote, wooded area with a ranger from the Scout camp and a detailed map.

"I saw the skull immediately," she says. "The back part, shining in the sunlight."

Enter the Missouri State Highway Patrol.

"When we arrived at the scene, the skull was lying on the ground," recalls Sgt. William Conway. "Other bones were scattered several hundred feet away from the gravesite."

Highway patrolmen inspected the area and sealed it off with barrier tape. Shortly after, they teamed with the county coroner, pathologist, and sheriff's department in excavating and collecting evidence from the shallow unmarked grave.

"It was a five- to six-day process," says Sgt. Don Bizelli. "We got down on our hands and knees and searched the entire area for anything we could find. Another officer and I even sifted through a dumptruck-load of dirt, trying to locate teeth to aid in identification."

Despite their efforts, few items were unearthed.

They found a skull, lower jaw, three- and four-inch strands of hair, tattered blue jeans, pieces of a flowered shirt, remnants of a plastic Service Merchandise shopping bag, a metal button with *Texwood* written across it, and about forty assorted bones, some of which had been chewed by animals.

That was all. No names. No numbers. No recognizable body.

Just bones, remnants, and a button with a mysterious logo.

Police detectives unearth a jawbone.

Combing the area for more clues

Police excavate and collect evidence from the unmarked grave, which has been sealed off with barrier tape.

Among the evidence they collect is a pelvic bone.

Interpreting Clues

After collecting the physical evidence, investigators forwarded it to the forensic crime lab for closer inspection.

Here key clues unfolded.

"By measuring the outer leg seam of the blue jeans, from the top of the waistband to the bottom of the cuff, we estimated the individual's height," Sergeant Conway says. "Weight was calculated from the waistband."

The blue-and-white plastic bag from Service Merchandise also proved significant. "The bag told us the body had been buried within recent years," he says. "This was *not*, for instance, an old Indian gravesite, which is very common around here."

The bag also helped police pinpoint the earliest possible date the body could have been abandoned.

"We went to the manufacturer, asked when they started using the logo printed on the bag, and found out it was 1979," Sergeant Conway says.

Hair collected at the scene, although badly decomposed, added information to the victim's profile. Analysis of its color and structure suggested the owner was Caucasian, or white, with dark brown hair.

This description supported the investigating team's belief that the skeletal remains belonged to a petite white woman.

When police pulled together enough details, they checked the information against the computer database of missing persons at the National Crime Information Center.

Several candidates fit the subject's general description, but each eventually was ruled out based on dental records. The Missouri victim's teeth were in good condition and showed no signs of fillings or dental work; the others did.

"We kept running into dead ends," Sergeant Bizelli says. "So I started looking

Sometimes the key clue to solving a crime is something that seems small and insignificant, like this button.

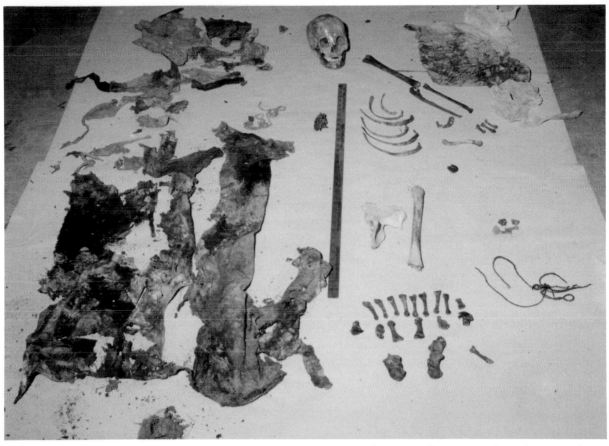

Back at the police station, detectives organize and photograph evidence collected at the scene. A yardstick or ruler is usually included in such photographs to indicate scale.

back and reading the lab reports for something new."

One item that particularly intrigued the patrolman was the metal button inscribed with the word *Texwood.*

"I called the lab and asked if they knew who manufactured Texwood jeans," he says. "They couldn't find it in their button file and told me to call the FBI's lab in Washington, D.C. They'd never heard of it either."

Now Sergeant Bizelli grew really curious. Somebody had to have information about this button. Determined to find it, he and Sergeant Conway spent five days calling button manufacturers in and around the United States and Canada.

Still no luck.

"Finally we called U.S. Customs. We figured if the manufacturer wasn't in the United States, it was overseas."

Bingo.

"Customs called back and said Texwood was the Levi Strauss of the Orient."

A company representative told Sergeant Bizelli that Texwood jeans were made in Hong Kong and sold exclusively in East Asia, because the firm designed them specifically for Asian builds.

"This indicated the individual had been to the Orient at one time, had contacts there, or possibly was of Asian descent," Sergeant Conway says.

If so, the field of possible identifications would narrow considerably.

The strategy now was to determine whether the victim was of Asian descent. The time had come to call in Dr. Michael Charney, the forensic anthropologist who could put together a "bone biography" by reading the once-living tissue that recorded this person's life.

Mouthful of Evidence

A plane crash. An unidentified body. And a five-million-dollar life insurance policy. Did the pilot really die, or is he faking his death for the insurance money?

That's one of the many questions forensic dentists can help police answer when they examine dental remains and compare them with a suspected victim's dental records.

"Our job is to help solve crimes using modern dental technology," says forensic dentist Dr. Robert Lorenz. "Sometimes we confirm the identification of murder victims. Other times, we help identify suspects in a crime by examining bite marks."

Everyone has a unique set of teeth. Some people have fillings, crowns, and/or chipped teeth that can aid in identification. In fact, forensic dentists have as many as 160 tooth surfaces — five on each tooth — that they can examine and compare with dental X rays and records. If all or some of the teeth are missing, the shape of different tooth sockets can be compared.

Bite marks also are useful in identification. Sometimes, criminals bite their victims in a fit of passion and leave behind incriminating evidence. Forensic dentists photograph and make plaster impressions of these marks to compare with the teeth of suspects. When a bite mark is old, forensic dentists shine ultraviolet light — light that's not visible to the human eye — on the wound so it will reflect areas that cannot be seen in ordinary light. The bite mark is then photographed and analyzed.

What can forensic dentists tell from a bite mark?

They can tell if the suspect had a big space between his teeth, and whether he has a tooth that's broken or missing. "We also can tell whether the person is large or small by measuring the distance between the two eye-teeth," Dr. Lorenz notes.

Even bite marks left in objects at the scene of a crime can be examined and compared. "We've taken impressions of bite marks from apples, cheese, candy bars, and bubble gum," says Dr. Lorenz. "Though bubble gum is a tough one."

Can you guess why?

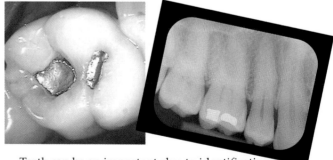

Teeth can be an important clue to identification because of their unique shape, size, and fillings. At right is an X ray of the tooth pictured above.

(Answer: Lots of bite marks!)

The Stories Bones Tell

June 1988: A cardboard box marked FRAGILE arrives at Dr. Charney's office. He's expecting it. Missouri State Highway Patrol investigators had called earlier requesting his help in identifying a skull and bones found at a Boy Scout camp.

Dr. Charney opens the package and carefully unwraps the skull and each bone. After identifying the specimens as human, he lays the remains on a wide wooden table and pieces together what's left of the person's skeleton.

"I do this to see what bones I have to tell the age, race, and so on," he explains.

This time, the Sherlock Holmes of skeletons doesn't have many: a skull and about forty small bones and fragments.

He picks up the skull and probes its nooks and crannies. Now he's ready to ask questions:

- *Do the remains belong to a man or a woman?*
- *How old was the person at the time of death?*
- *Was he or she short, tall, or of average height?*
- *Are signs of violence present?*
- *What about anomalies, healed fractures, or other distinctive markers?*

Only the bone detective's trained eye can discern the answers to these questions.

By inspecting the skull alone, Dr. Charney collects clues to a person's identity.

"Male skulls are generally larger and heavier than female skulls," he notes. The skull sent by Missouri police was small and lightly developed.

Male skulls also tend to have a bony ridge above their eyes. The Missouri skull didn't.

Neither did it display the relatively low, slanted forehead or smooth upper eye rim typically seen in males.

Dr. Charney measures a skull with spreading calipers.

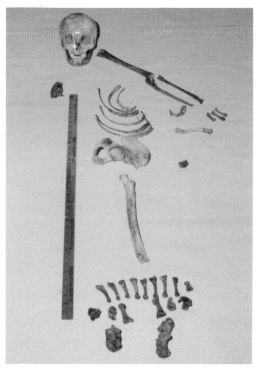
A victim's bones are carefully laid out during the identification process.

Its facial features rounded at the forehead and sharpened around the top of the upper eye rim.

Still, how could Dr. Charney be positive these remains belonged to a woman?

The best way to know for certain is by examining the pubic bones, which sit in the front of the pelvis, or hipbone. In general, a woman's pelvis is proportionally wider than a man's, making room for childbearing.

By measuring the size of an angle formed by the pubic bone called the subpubic angle, Dr. Charney can determine whether the bones belong to a man or a woman.

"If the angle measures less than 90 degrees, it's a male. If it measures more than 90 degrees, it's a female."

The pubic bones communicate other things as well. For example, when a mother-to-be is in labor, the pubic bones will separate to allow additional room for the baby's head. After a woman has delivered two children, the process leaves a small indentation on the bones, Dr. Charney says.

The Missouri specimen measured 100 degrees at the subpubic angle. A depression was also visible on the pubic bone.

Dr. Charney's conclusion: The victim was a woman who had given birth to at least two children.

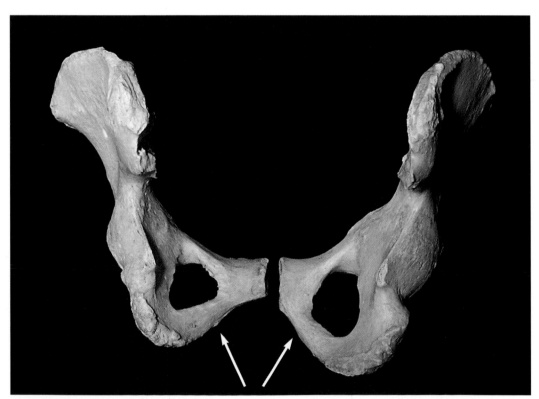

The subpubic angle, an angle formed by the pubic bone, is generally wider in women (*left*) and steeper in men (*right*). Can you see the difference?

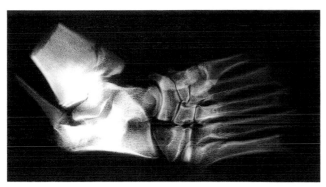

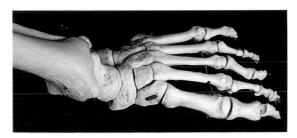

A bear paw, shown in an X ray at left, is so similar to a human's foot (*right*) that the two are often mistaken for each other, especially when the toes are missing.

"Bear" Bones

Pig bones. Sheep bones. Cow bones. Deer bones. Forensic anthropologist Doug Owsley at the Smithsonian Institution has seen them all come through his laboratory.

"It's not uncommon for people to mistake animal bones for human bones," he says. In fact, it's easy to do when remains have been partially burned in a fire or chewed by animals.

That's why the first thing bone detectives do when examining remains is to decide whether they're human.

In June 1990, Maryland police brought Dr. Owsley a partially skeletonized right foot. Held together by ligaments, the specimen included an ankle, heel, and other foot bones. A dog had discovered the remains while wandering from its home, and authorities worried the specimen was human.

"Structurally it looked like a human foot," Dr. Owsley says, especially since the toe bones were missing. But closer examination revealed the foot to be the hind paw of an adult black bear.

"Apparently the bear had been killed and the paws removed during the process of skinning," he says.

Among the key features distinguishing the bear paw from a human foot was the width of the heel bone. A bear paw's heel is narrower (and relatively longer) than a human's.

The length of the metatarsals, or the bones at the arch of the foot, also provided clues to identification.

The longest metatarsal in a human is nearest the big toe, Dr. Owsley says, while the longest equivalent in a bear is closer to the baby toe.

"That's because humans tend to put more weight on the inside of the foot and bears put more weight on the outside."

To recognize these variations in species, an observer must have extensive experience working with bones, Dr. Owsley says. This is why it's often difficult for police and others to identify partial remains. "They're just not used to seeing the subtle differences."

Ancestral Ties

Once he's determined the sex of the victim, Dr. Charney moves to another important identifying clue: race.

"Racial differences are best observed in the facial features of the skull," he says, lifting a specimen to demonstrate.

"Caucasians typically have narrow faces with long, high-bridged nasal bones, while blacks generally have broader nose bridges and jaws that slope outward."

People of the Mongoloid race — Eskimos, American Indians, and those native to Asia — usually have short, broad faces with squared, winglike cheekbones, he adds.

"The difference in bone structure evolved from our ancestors' adaptation to different climates and environments," Dr. Charney explains. "The most challenging skulls to identify are those from people of mixed races."

In the Missouri case, the victim's race was especially important because police suspected an Asian connection. If the woman was Asian, it would narrow their search considerably. If she was Caucasian, they would continue trying to identify a small white woman.

Unaware of it at the time, Dr. Charney supported police detectives' suspicions in his conclusions.

After taking careful measurements, the bone expert found the skull to have a broad face with squared, winglike cheekbones and a small, low-bridged nasal bone — all characteristics of the Mongoloid race.

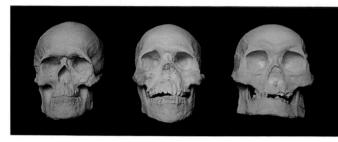

Left to right: Plaster casts of Caucasian, Negroid, and Mongoloid skulls. Notice the differences in facial structure.

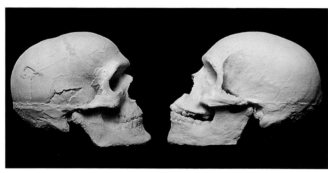

Caucasian skulls, such as the one on the left, feature high-bridged nasal bones, while Negroid skulls display broader nose bridges as well as outward sloping jaws.

Fingered

Fingerprints have been a powerful crime-fighting tool for more than a century. That's because no two are ever alike. (No wonder some criminals try to burn theirs off!)

Until recently, however, fingerprints lifted at a crime scene were virtually useless to police, unless they had a suspect's prints to check against. Manually searching through thousands of file cards for suspects involved hundreds of hours and would have taken years just to match one set of prints.

Today it's a matter of minutes with AFIS — Automated Fingerprint Identification System.

AFIS is a high-speed computer system that stores fingerprint images and maps information about the patterns of loops, whorls, and arches distinguishing each person's print. After AFIS records the data, it compares the information against millions of prints on file and pulls up a list of potential candidates for experts to verify visually.

"That's the advantage of the system," says latent fingerprint examiner Bob Stratton. "Before AFIS, detectives submitted suspects for us to check out. Now we can come up with suspects for officers to investigate."

The new technology helps crack old cases, too.

In California, AFIS fingered a man for murder thirty years after the crime was committed, and a jury sent him to prison for life.

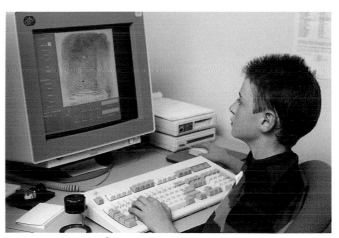

A visitor to the Denver Police Lab explores the AFIS computer system. AFIS helps police classify and compare thousands of fingerprints in a matter of minutes (instead of hundreds of hours).

No Bone Unturned

Determining race and sex helps Dr. Charney write the first few chapters of a person's bone biography. But now it's time to narrow down the investigation and fill in the story with details.

How old was the victim at the time of death? How much did he or she weigh? What was his or her height?

Age markers — at least the best ones — are not typically found on the skull. They are buried in other bones.

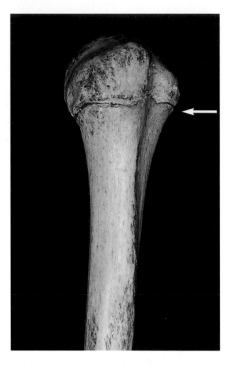

- *In children under thirteen, one of the most reliable age indicators is in the developing wrist, Dr. Charney says. Babies' wrists are made of a rubbery substance called cartilage, which slowly turns to bone in a predictable sequence as they grow older. With a wrist X ray, a child's age can be estimated within a few months. Another common method of calculating age in young children is to look at tooth formation and eruption patterns, which also follow a standard sequence.*

While teens are growing, the knobbed ends of their long bones are separated from the mid-portion, or shaft, by cartilage (*above*). When they reach full growth, the cartilage turns to bone and the bone ends fuse with the shaft (*below*).

- *In teens, the knobbed ends of long bones — such as the femur, or thighbone — are the best places to pinpoint age. By noting the degree to which the ends are fused to the shaft, or middle, of the bone, Dr. Charney can estimate the age of a specimen through young adulthood.*

- *For adults up to fifty-five, one of the best age indicators lies in an area where the pubic bones meet in front of the pelvis. Young people have bumps and ridges on the surface, but these gradually smooth out in phases as they grow older.*

- *Beyond age fifty-five, signs of arthritis at the joints and spine provide clues to age. Osteon counting, a special, more time-consuming technique used on bones from all age groups, also works. With the help of a microscope, a forensic expert can examine a cross section of bone and count its osteons, the tiny tunnels in bone that house nutrient-providing blood*

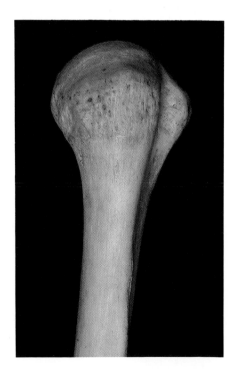

vessels and nerves. In general, the more osteons and fragments of osteons, the older the person.

As for the Missouri case, the best bones for predicting age were all damaged or missing, so Dr. Charney extracted information elsewhere. By examining the development of the collarbone, he could tell the victim was probably older than twenty-two.

He also noted that the cranial sutures — the place where the skull bones permanently join — were closed. These wiggly lines on the dome of the skull usually begin to close when people are in their mid-twenties, so Dr. Charney figured the victim had been at least that old.

To confirm his findings and narrow down the age range, he moved on to the teeth.

"Based on the degree of gum recession and wear and tear on the teeth, we arrived at the age of twenty-five, give or take a few years."

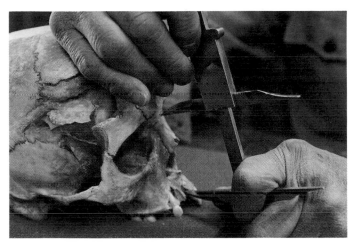

Measuring the upper facial height in relation to width enables Dr. Charney to determine whether a person had a broad or narrow face.

Measuring Up

Next, Dr. Charney calculates the victim's height. Even when many bones are missing, it's still possible to estimate a person's stature.

How? In this case, he focused on one of the victim's long limb bones. He measured the radius, or the main forearm bone, on an osteometric board and entered the number into a special mathematical equation. Developed from the bones of people whose height is already known, this formula allows researchers to estimate the stature of a person based on a single bone.

The results: The unidentified woman from Missouri stood at about five feet.

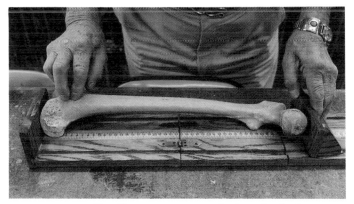

Dr. Charney measures the length of a femur, or thighbone, to estimate a person's height.

Tipping the Scales

Height is easier to pinpoint than weight.

"Unfortunately rolls of fat and 'rubber tires' around our waists leave no markings on bone," Dr. Charney says.

Despite this, he is one of the bone detectives who attempt to give police a rough estimate of weight. He bases his predictions on:

• *the person's sex and height*
• *the skeleton's frame size: small, medium, or large*
• *muscle attachment markings on the bone*

"One reason I look at the muscle markings is to see if the muscles have been used or not," he says.

In living people, bone responds to muscles connected to it with the help of tissue called tendons. The more a person uses a muscle, the rougher the bone's surface becomes to anchor the tendons.

Well-developed muscles tell Dr. Charney a couple of things. First, they indicate a person may have weighed more than average because muscle weighs more than fat. Second, they sometimes provide clues to a person's occupation.

Was the victim an athlete or construction worker? Forensic anthropologists can often tell depending on the number and location of the muscle markings. Such markings may also provide clues as to whether a person was left- or right-handed.

In the Missouri case, the victim was a five-foot-tall woman with a small frame and smooth-surfaced bones, indicating she wasn't particularly muscular in the areas represented. Armed with this information, Dr. Charney consulted a medical weight chart and concluded the victim weighed 120 pounds, plus or minus five pounds.

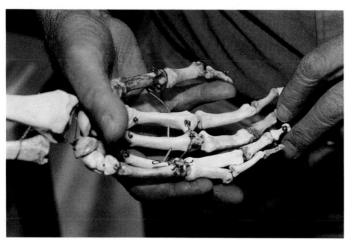

Forensic anthropologists can sometimes tell whether a person was left- or right-handed by examining his or her bones.

Anthropometry, the study of human body measurement, in action

Bone-Boggler

One story Dr. Charney likes to tell students involves a forensic anthropologist who arrived at a woman's occupation by reading her bones.

Soon after the bone detective received the skeleton to examine, she noticed that the muscle attachment markings on the right shoulder were especially rough with grainy ridges. This indicated the woman probably had spent a lot of time carrying some type of weight above her shoulder.

What occupation involves continuously supporting weight above one shoulder? Dr. Charney asks visitors.

"Postal worker?"

"Mother, carrying a baby?"

"Professional with a briefcase?"

These are a few responses Dr. Charney receives. What do you think? All of the above? None of the above? See how long it takes you to figure out this bone-boggling question.

(Answer: Waitress)

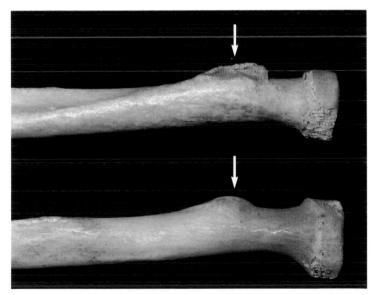

Note the difference between the surfaces of the muscle attachment points on these bones. A rough surface (*top*) indicates the muscle in that area was well developed; a smooth surface (*bottom*) indicates it was not.

Written in Bone

Once Dr. Charney establishes a preliminary profile of a person, he searches for distinguishing features on the bones that will help identify the victim.

Luckily everyone's skeletal frame is unique. Sometimes heredity carves out distinctive markers. Other times, important events such as injuries, illnesses, and childbearing etch their imprint. To the bone detective, each inscription is another clue to identifying the unknown.

In some cases, anomalies such as a bone spur help pinpoint the identity of a person.

Sinus prints, healed fractures, and the zigzagged cranial sutures that join the bones of the skull also make for one-of-a-kind markers. When medical X rays from reported victims are available, these items are easy for a bone detective to compare and often lead to identification. (The key is to come up with a likely victim!)

While examining the few remains of the Missouri woman, Dr. Charney found evidence of violence.

Many times, stab wounds, bullet holes, and blows to the head leave their signature on bones and indicate a likely cause of death. A break in the U-shaped hyoid bone in the center of the throat, for example, suggests that a person died of strangulation.

The Missouri bones didn't show such obvious signs of violence, but Dr. Charney did notice a small fracture on the back of the skull.

"It was a little hole that looked as if she'd hit something," he says. An X ray of the skull revealed that the woman received the wound around the time of death (perimortem) and not after. This was evident from the twisted nature of the fracture.

"Bone is living tissue," Dr. Charney explains. "If you break it, it tears the same way a fresh twig breaks, in a sort of stringy, uneven manner. A dead twig, on the other hand, will snap right away, as will dead bone."

What did this small fracture mean? The bone detective would soon find out.

A bullet penetrated this skull.

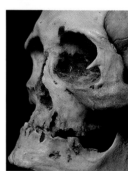

Bone spurs, such as the one projecting from this eye socket, can help forensic experts identify victims.

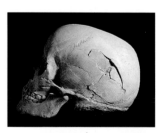

A blow to the head with a rock left a cracked skull.

A sword sliced through this skull 4,500 years ago.

FORENSIC FILE

Invisible Clues

Deoxyribonucleic acid. Not easy to say or see. But DNA, as it's more commonly called, contains the secret code to who we are. Coiled within the cells of our body, DNA's genetic instructions dictate whether our eyes are blue or brown, our hair is blond or black — even whether we're a boy or a girl.

Because each person's DNA pattern differs (except in the case of identical twins), we carry a microscopic identification card wherever we go. This invisible ID card can be extracted from cells in blood, skin, hair, saliva, bones, and even tooth pulp.

When criminals leave behind traces of body fluids and tissues at the scene of a crime, they give detectives a genetic clue to their identity.

Using a revolutionary technique known as DNA profiling, forensic scientists can compare cell samples collected at a crime scene with those of a suspect and determine whether they come from the same person.

Postage stamps, sweatbands, envelope flaps, and cigarette butts are just a few places detectives have found incriminating tissue samples.

"DNA typing adds one more piece of evidence to the crime-solving puzzle," says Jeanne Kilmer, a forensic serologist at the Denver, Colorado, police crime lab. "In some cases, it clears suspects and allows detectives to redirect their investigation."

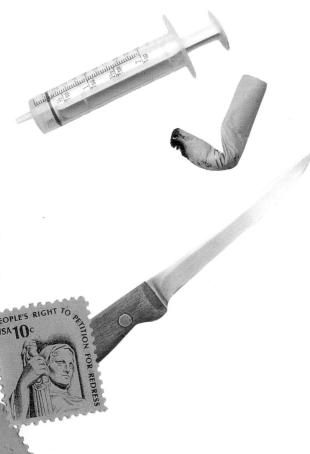

Skeletal Sculptures

Forensic sculptor Nita Bitner begins a facial restoration by cutting round rubber pegs into different lengths.

* Nita Bitner resculpted the face of the Missouri woman for this book; Angela Nelson molded the original for the case (shown on page 35).

Up till now, Dr. Charney's expertise in forensic anthropology has enabled him to take a few pieces of a skeleton and compile a portrait of a five-foot, 120-pound Asian woman in her mid-twenties. Still, that isn't enough to identify her.

The dead woman's "face" needs to be brought back to life.

Reconstructing the likeness of a person in clay, using the skull as a guide, is a last resort at identification, Dr. Charney says. It gives police a new lead to follow, a visual clue that can be photographed and displayed in the media so that others can help solve the mystery.

Facial reconstruction, in itself, is not an identifying tool, he warns. The goal is to trigger someone to recognize the clay model and to then identify the person through scientific means.

"All that's needed is a general recognition that it looks like so-and-so," he says. "After that, you can go to the family, see if someone's missing, and proceed from there."

Before re-creating a face, Dr. Charney and forensic sculptor Nita Bitner* search the skull for signs of disease, injury, and structural defects.

"We look for things that shouldn't be there," Bitner says. "Sometimes we find broken noses, cuts, or dentures." These affect the face's appearance and aid in the identification process. If the nose bone is curved to one side, for example, it's important to show it in the face because it's a distinguishing feature.

"We have to be careful, however, not to include anything that happened at the time of death," Bitner notes, "because it wouldn't be recognizable to others."

Age also influences how a face is built. Wrinkled skin, which might help illustrate an older person, is often incorporated into a sculpture for accuracy.

After studying the Missouri woman's skull, Bitner makes a latex mold and pours a plaster cast. Now she's ready to sculpt the face.

First, she cuts thirty round rubber pegs into various lengths and glues them to the skull. Each peg, called a landmark, represents the thickness of the soft tissue (composed of muscle, fat, and skin) at different points on the face and helps her sculpt along the blueprint of the bone. These tissue depths, which differ for men and women of varying ages, were first calculated from corpses by nineteenth-century scientists and later updated.

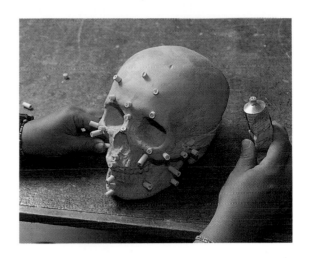

Next Bitner connects the dotlike pegs with modeling clay. Starting at the forehead, she carefully works her way to the cheekbones, nasal area, chin, and mouth.

"I follow the face and do what it tells me to do," she says.

Once the "dots" are connected, Bitner fills in the spaces between the crisscrossing strips of clay and fleshes out the face. Now the prominent cheekbones of the Missouri woman become strikingly clear. Suddenly her broad face and delicate nose emerge.

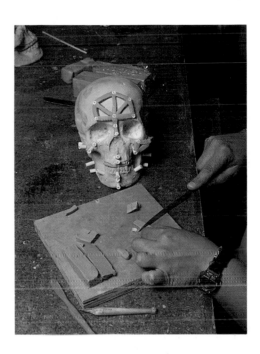

As Bitner smooths the clay with her thumbs, the face develops like a photograph. When she sets the plastic brown eyes in their sockets and bends the lids around them, the sculpture springs to life.

After the front profile is complete, Bitner molds the ears and pats the face with a damp sponge. This lends a natural, textured look to the sculpture's "skin."

Because the Missouri woman is presumed to be Asian, Bitner adorns the model with a black wig and adds a scarf for a finishing touch.

The model is now ready to be photographed and publicized in the media so that millions of amateur detectives can help solve the riddle of her identity.

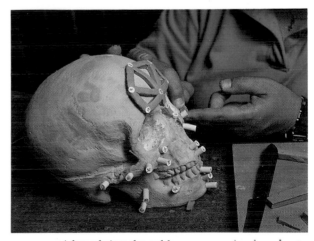

After gluing the rubber pegs, or landmarks, to the skull cast, Bitner "connects the dots" with strips of modeling clay.

When attaching the strips of clay, Bitner begins at the forehead and works her way down to the cheekbones, nasal area, chin, and mouth.

Once the landmarks are connected, Bitner fills in the spaces with clay and fleshes out the face.

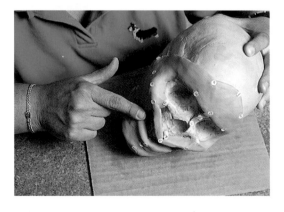

As Bitner smooths the clay with her fingers, a portrait of the victim begins to emerge.

Bitner sets the plastic brown eyes in their sockets.

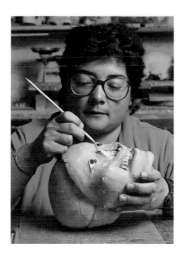

Next come the eyelids.

Bitner then sculpts the sides of the nose.

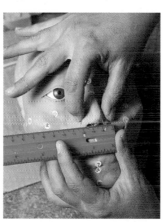

She measures the nose with a ruler to ensure it is the correct width.

Now its time to mold the upper lip.

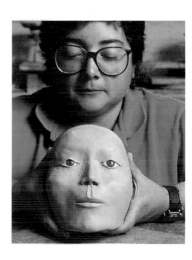

The face is nearly complete. Soon Bitner will add a scarf and a wig to make the sculpture more recognizable.

FORENSIC FILE

A fly's predictable life cycle can help solve crimes.

Bugged

They buzz, bite, and bother. But bugs can help solve crimes, too.

How? By leading predictable lives.

Within hours after a person dies, waves of insects swarm to the scene. Here creatures such as blowflies feed, lay eggs, and pass through distinct stages of growth. (The blowfly changes from egg to larva to pupa before it emerges as an adult.)

By examining these insects and tracing back to when their eggs were laid, forensic entomologists can arrive at a likely time of death.

The lone presence of blowfly eggs or first-stage larvae tells investigators a body has been exposed twenty-four hours or less; older maggots suggest that a corpse has been decaying a few days to a couple of weeks, depending on the air temperatures.

When no bugs are present — which is extremely rare in the warm months of the year — it may indicate the body has been frozen and just recently abandoned.

Time of death isn't all insects buzz about. Other bug behaviors provide different clues.

For example, when insects that lay eggs only outdoors are discovered on a body found in a building, investigators may suspect someone moved the victim. The same holds true when bugs native to one area of the country are suspiciously discovered in

another. Some species even reveal during what season a crime occurred and whether it happened during the day or night.

Insects have been bugging criminals for thousands of years, says forensic entomologist Boris Kondratieff. In the thirteenth century, bugs helped solve the mysterious slashing murder of a Chinese villager.

After routine attempts to track the killer failed, authorities called local farmers to line up with their sickles beside them. Attracted to the scent of blood, flies immediately clustered to one of the blades. Soon after, the owner broke down and confessed.

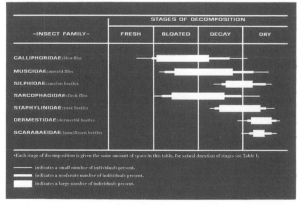

Different kinds of insects invade a decaying body at various stages of decomposition.

The Face Is Familiar

October 24, 1988: The State Highway Patrol releases photos of the Missouri woman's facial restoration to television and newspaper reporters. "The victim was buried in a shallow grave at a Boy Scout camp," reads the attached notice. "Anyone who can identify the woman . . . should call Sergeant Bizelli or Sergeant Conway at the Highway Patrol."

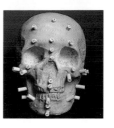

Three days later, the phone rings.

"The photo in the newspaper looks like a friend my wife and I haven't seen in several years," a man tells Sergeant Conway. "Her name is Bun Chee Nyhuis, and she's a native of Thailand."

The caller continues. He says Mrs. Nyhuis's husband told him that Bun Chee had left him and returned to Thailand. But the caller and his wife had found it hard to believe that Mrs. Nyhuis would leave without telling them. Now, after seeing the photo, they are really worried about their friend.

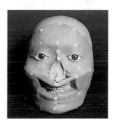

Police record the information and contact Mrs. Nyhuis's husband, Richard.

"He told us the same story," Sergeant Conway says. "He said Bun Chee left him in December 1983 and the last time he saw her was at St. Louis Airport. That's why he didn't report her missing."

Sergeant Conway didn't believe the alibi, but he didn't have any proof the man was lying. Besides, no one had reported Mrs. Nyhuis missing, and he wasn't even sure she was the unidentified woman.

He called the bone detective to discuss the new development.

"Send me a photo of her," Dr. Charney said. "I'll superimpose it over the skull and see if it matches."

Police sent Dr. Charney two photos of Mrs. Nyhuis. One was rejected because she was looking down and the view of her face was limited. The other pictured her clowning around, playfully sticking out her tongue.

A sculpture springs to life.

This unusual pose made the superimposition more difficult for the bone detective, but not impossible.

Using 35-millimeter slides of the skull and the photograph, Dr. Charney projected the slide of the skull over the picture of the woman.

Unlike previous photos that had been sent to Dr. Charney's office for study, the photo of Mrs. Nyhuis fit perfectly with the image of the skull. The forehead, cheeks, chin, and nasal bone all snapped into place.

Mrs. Nyhuis also fit the profile Dr. Charney had developed by reading her bones: She was a petite thirty-three-year-old Asian mother of two who was about five feet tall.

"That's her," Dr. Charney told police. "This skull belongs to the woman in the photograph."

A photograph sent to Dr. Charney by police for superimposition

A projected photograph of the victim's skull

The two images fit together, indicating a match.

Witness from the Grave

With Dr. Charney's identification of Bun Chee Nyhuis, Missouri police began searching for evidence linking Richard Nyhuis to the murder of his wife.

They checked with neighbors: Yes, the Nyhuises had had a stormy relationship and quarreled often.

They checked with his employer: Yes, Mr. Nyhuis had requested a few days off in December 1983, telling supervisors his wife had left him.

He'd also removed his wife as beneficiary of his insurance policy and divorced her.

"Then we found out he was very active in the Boy Scouts, and everything fell into place," Sergeant Conway says. "That's when it became clear why the body was buried in the middle of nowhere at this Scout camp."

On July 17, 1989, police confronted Mr. Nyhuis near the area where his wife's remains were found. At first, Mr. Nyhuis stuck to the original story about his wife's disappearance. But after police pointed out several discrepancies, he broke down and confessed to killing her. Still, he insisted, it was an accident. He pushed her during an argument, he said, and she fell and hit her head on the base of a steel post. (That's where the fracture in the back of the skull had come from!)

Nyhuis went on to admit that after his wife died, he hid her body in a basement freezer until the spring of 1984, when he buried her at the Boy Scout ranch.

"He said the ranch was the most remote area he knew," says Sergeant Bizelli.

The case went to trial, and Dr. Charney took the stand as an expert witness. Using slides, photos, and bone displays, the forensic anthropologist explained his findings to the court for more than three hours.

As events of the trial unfolded, the clay model of Bun Chee Nyhuis — now exhibited

Newspapers such as the *St. Louis Post-Dispatch* covered the Nyhuis case from the time the bones were discovered at the Boy Scout ranch until Richard Nyhuis was convicted of murder.

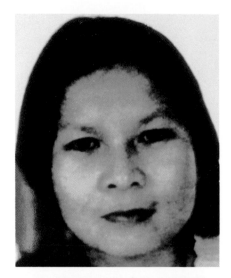

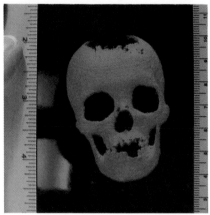

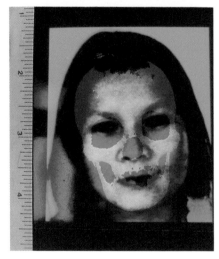

After Mrs. Nyhuis was identified as the probable victim in the Missouri case, police sent her immigration photo to Dr. Charney. The bone detective did a second skull/photograph superimposition using a computer, a laser, and special software. The immigration photograph and digitized skull superimposed for a perfect fit.

as evidence — eerily stood watch. "It was the only murder case I've tried where the victim came face-to-face with the accused in the courtroom," says prosecuting attorney Tim Braun.

Thanks to the testimony of the bone detective and other experts, it took a jury only two hours to find Richard Nyhuis guilty of first-degree murder. Today he's serving a life sentence without parole in a Missouri state prison.

Sergeants Conway and Bizelli, on the other hand, have moved on to new cases, where they continue to "pit their minds against people who've committed the ultimate crime."

Still, they'll never forget the Nyhuis case.

"The Bun Chee Nyhuis case was extremely rare," explains Sergeant Conway. "It's the only one like it I've been involved with in my career. The odds of digging up remains this old and then identifying them and getting an arrest and conviction are pretty slim."

Police credit teamwork and Dr. Charney for their success.

"There were lots of pieces to the jigsaw puzzle that made it work," Sergeant Conway says. Among those were:

- *the man from Finland who found the remains*
- *the investigators who sifted the ground for evidence*
- *the crime lab that analyzed the evidence for clues*
- *the officer who discovered that the Texwood button was manufactured in Hong Kong*

All these developments led to Dr. Charney in Colorado, who pulled together a profile of the victim and built a clay model of her face that was eventually identified, says Sergeant Conway.

"If it wasn't for that model, her friends — and the rest of us — may never have known what became of her."

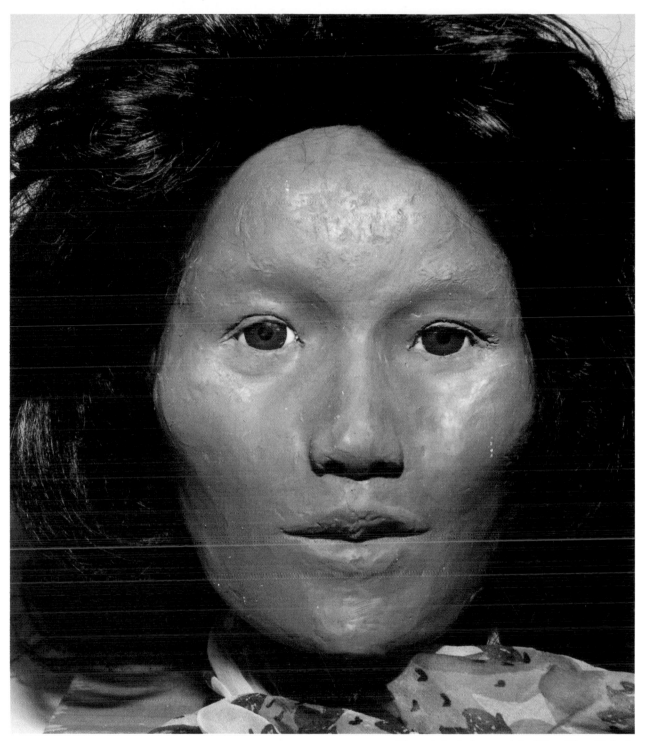

The original clay model of Bun Chee Nyhuis eerily stood watch at the trial.

Bones communicate many things about who people are and how they may have died. But reading bones also helps us discover who we once were and how our most distant relatives lived.

"Lucy," a 3.2-million-year-old fossil, surprised many researchers with information about our ancient ancestors soon after she was unearthed in 1974.

Discovered within Ethiopia's Afar region, tiny Lucy stood at about three feet six inches and weighed only sixty-five pounds as an adult. Most intriguing was the rounded shape of her pelvis and the anatomy of her leg and foot bones. These told researchers that unlike most mammals, who move on four limbs, Lucy walked in an upright position, just as

OLD BONES

Lucy's Legacy

The three-million-year-old fossil skull shown above, of an adult male nicknamed "the son of Lucy," offers insights into what our ancient ancestors may have looked like.

humans do. Finding Lucy indicated to scientists that this important skeletal change had occurred hundreds of thousands of years earlier than scientists had previously believed.

The discovery led to the naming of a new tongue-twisting species called *Australopithecus afarensis,* or *A. afarensis* for short. Many believe this species is one of humankind's earliest known ancestors and close to the root of the human family tree.

In 1992, almost twenty years after finding Lucy, researchers uncovered more fossils from the *A. afarensis* family, including the first nearly complete skull of an adult male nicknamed "the son of Lucy."

The three-million-year-old skull, pieced together from more than two hundred rock-encrusted fragments, offers new insights and confirms a lot of what researchers suspected, says Dr. Eric Meikle of the Institute of Human Origins in Berkeley, California.

The small brain, large face, and flat forehead attest to the species' apelike qualities from the neck up.

The large jutting jaw, well-worn teeth, and signs of strong chewing muscles suggest Lucy and her family were mainly vegetarians. Most likely, they snacked on fruits, vegetables, insects, and small animals.

"If they did kill anything, it probably wasn't very big," Dr. Meikle says, "since there's no evidence of tools or weapons. It's possible they also collected eggs, which is another form of predation."

Along with information gleaned from the skull, researchers pieced together data from other fossils in Lucy's species.

One thing they discovered is that *A. afarensis* had long, strong arm bones with relatively large muscle attachment markings. This may indicate they spent a lot of time climbing trees, even though they were bipeds, primarily walking on two feet.

Another revelation was the substantial size difference between males and females in the species.

While Lucy and other female *A. afarensis* specimens averaged about three-and-a-half feet tall, males appear to have been four-and-a-half to five feet tall, based on the size of their limbs. Males also weighed up to twice as much as females, averaging 100 to 130 pounds.

"The difference is much more than in modern humans and more like that of gorillas and orangutans," Dr. Meikle says.

It's this combination of characteristics that makes Lucy's family unique.

"Clearly they're not just small humans with small brains," Dr. Meikle explains. "They are something different."

"If you saw them walking at a distance, you might think they were children. You wouldn't think they were apes. But if you moved closer and saw their faces, you'd see a lot of apelike traits."

Despite this, scientists maintain *A. afarensis*'s upright posture ties them to humans.

"No other kind of animal has ever moved around like we do," Dr. Meikle says. "Their anatomy from the waist down makes it clear they're related to us much more closely than to living or fossil apes."

illions of years after Lucy and her family walked the earth, a lone mountaineer lay down to die high in the Alps. Preserved naturally by deep snows and glacial ice, the voyager settled in the icy grave for 5,300 years. On September 19, 1991, hikers along the Austrian-Italian border stumbled upon his shriveled corpse.

The discovery turned out to be one of the most important archaeological finds of the century. The "Iceman" opened a window to the past, providing clues about life in Europe's Copper Age around the year 3000 B.C.

"Stones and bones" are what you generally find from this time period, says John Gurche, an artist and anthropologist who has studied the Iceman.

OLD BONES
The Iceman Comes to Life

A recovery team removes the Iceman from his frozen grave in the Alps.

Archaeologists usually dig up skeletons, not soft tissue, he says. They also tend to find ritual materials buried with a person, instead of the accessories of everyday life.

Not this time.

At five feet two inches tall, the oldest intact mummy still has his ears, eyes, brain, and other internal organs.

"He also has tattoos in several places, something that wouldn't even have been speculated about without the preservation of the soft tissue," Gurche says.

Making the find even more exceptional is the survival equipment found near the Iceman's body. Among the items discovered were a flint dagger, a set of unfinished arrows, an unstrung bow, a deerskin quiver, and a copper ax. These, along with the Iceman's layered animal-skin clothing, grass cape, and leather shoes, helped scientists paint an image of the ancient traveler's world.

Now people wondered: What did he look like?

To find out, the National Geographic Society commissioned Gurche to reconstruct the Iceman's face, using forensic identification techniques.

Typically a facial restoration begins with the skull. But in this case, the skull was still inside the body, so Gurche had to build his own.

Using information and measurements from X rays, CAT scans, and other available data, Gurche designed a skull in clay and cast it in plastic.

Before sculpting the face, he considered the Iceman's sex, race, age, and body build. This helped him decide which "flesh," or soft-tissue thickness indicators, to follow.

"The closest data set was the one for European males, ages seventeen to forty, medium build," he says. "That's what's represented in the rubber pegs."

As Gurche built the face with clay, he noted other skeletal clues: the broad forehead, humped nose, slight underbite, prominent chin, and pronounced muscle markings in the jaw. All were incorporated into the features of the face.

When time came to add the glass eyes, he checked the Iceman's records for size and color.

"The eyes as they're now preserved are blue-gray," he explains. "The big question is: Were they the same color back then?"

Scientists may never be sure, but blue-gray is a common eye color in the Tyrolean Alps today.

After completing the facial restoration, Gurche took his creation a step further.

"I wanted to make it absolutely lifelike," he says.

To achieve his goal, Gurche created a cast of the clay head he'd made for the facial reconstruction using specially tinted urethane plastic. He then adorned it with a full head of human hair, punching in one strand at a time!

"Fortunately samples from the head and beard were recovered at the site," he says. "They told us his hair was dark brown to black, fairly wavy, and about three-and-a-half inches long at the max."

The result is hauntingly real.

Artist-anthropologist John Gurche's facial reconstruction of the Iceman

On June 25, 1876, Lt. Col. George Armstrong Custer and more than two hundred of his men died at the hands of Sioux and Cheyenne Indians in the bloody Battle of Little Bighorn — otherwise known as "Custer's Last Stand."

One hundred and seven years later, in August 1983, a prairie fire burned away much of the battlefield, giving archaeologists the opportunity to search for bones and artifacts still present at the site. Among the items recovered were scores of bullets, cartridge cases, and the partial skeletons of thirty-four men.

One set of remains that particularly intrigued forensic anthropologist Dr. Clyde Snow of Oklahoma included fragments of a skull, finger, and tailbone, along with eight teeth.

OLD BONES
Bones on the Battlefield

Skull fragments found at the site of the Battle of Little Bighorn fit perfectly (*above*) over the 1874 photograph of Custer's half-Indian scout, Mitch Boyer, shown at right.

These skeletal remains, Dr. Snow concluded, belonged to a man who died between the ages of thirty-five and forty-five. Judging from the fracture in his skull, the man most likely received a crushing blow to the head. Dr. Snow also noted that the victim's teeth were worn in an arched pattern, indicating he probably smoked a pipe.

What fascinated the bone detective most, however, was the man's racial identification. His facial bones, the best indicators of race, displayed characteristics of two groups. A wide nasal opening and large cheekbones suggested Indian ancestors, but other features indicated a Caucasian heritage.

Adding to the mystery was a mother-of-pearl shirt button found with the bones. The button suggested the individual was wearing civilian clothes when he died instead of a uniform.

Only one man under Custer's command could have fit that description: Mitch Boyer, a thirty-eight-year-old half-Indian scout, son of a Sioux mother and a French father.

To determine whether the bones belonged to Boyer, archaeologist Doug Scott of the National Park Service turned to superimposition. With the help of a television monitor, video cameras, and a dissolve unit, he overlaid images of the victim's facial bones with the only known photo of Mitch Boyer.

The facial fragments fit.

The partial orbit of the left eye and the cheekbone below it locked into place over Boyer's photo. The nasal cavity matched the scout's nose, and the teeth fit his mouth.

"We tried it on a couple of other photos," Scott says, to make sure it wasn't a fluke, "but there was just no way we could make it match. We even tried it on somebody who had a big, broad face like Mitch Boyer, but it wouldn't work."

Scientifically speaking, no one can be absolutely sure the bones identified belong to Mitch Boyer. But the odds are in his favor.

"There is one chance in a hundred this is not Boyer," Scott says. "But for the bones to match the photograph that well, it would almost have to be his twin brother."

Steely-eyed Jesse James and his brother Frank are considered two of the most notorious outlaws in American history. From 1866 to 1881, the pair robbed banks and trains in the Missouri area and killed anyone who got in their way.

The terror ended April 3, 1882.

On that morning, twenty-year-old Robert Ford shot and killed Jesse James for a $10,000 reward.

Jesse was buried near an old coffee bean tree in the backyard of his mother's Missouri farmhouse. His mom wanted him close by because she feared grave robbers might steal his body.

OLD BONES
Outlaw Rides Again

For twenty years, Mrs. Zerelda Samuel watched over her son's grave. In 1902 she decided it was safe to move Jesse to a local cemetery.

On the rainy morning of June 29, 1902, grave diggers exhumed Jesse's body while his son, Jesse Jr., stood by to identify the remains. When the coffin was lifted out of the ground, the bottom fell out along with Jesse's clothed skeleton.

The men retrieved the bones, and Jesse Jr. inspected them. A bullet hole in the skull and gold fillings in the teeth reassured young Jesse the skeleton belonged to his father. The crew moved the corpse to a new coffin and reburied the old casket in its original farmhouse grave.

The James family kept their famous farmhouse until 1978, when the county bought it. Soon after, officials ordered an excavation of Jesse James's old grave so that it could be

Here lies the body of Jesse James, one of the most notorious outlaws in American history.

restored as a historic site.

When archaeologists dug up the grave, however, they discovered it wasn't empty. Bones, hair, and a tooth remained.

Did they belong to Jesse James?

To find out, the county sent the specimens to Dr. Michael Finnegan, a forensic anthropologist at Kansas State University in Manhattan, Kansas. Without revealing the origins of the bones, officials asked Dr. Finnegan to glean information about the owner.

This was a challenge.

First he identified some of the bones as animals' and separated them from the human specimens. That left him with a neck vertebra, a canine tooth, two pieces of a skull, three toe bones, and some hair embedded in dirt.

Next he measured the length of the tooth and the width of the vertebra and determined that the bones most likely belonged to a man. Generally a man has a longer canine tooth than a woman and a wider vertebra.

The tooth also was key to estimating the person's age at the time of death. By cutting it in half and examining its structure, Dr. Finnegan calculated the owner's age to be about thirty-eight when he died, give or take 3.6 years.

Another detail Dr. Finnegan noted about the tooth was a defect in its crown called hypoplasia. When a tooth is developing, a long illness with a high fever can disrupt the formation of enamel surrounding it. After the fever breaks, normal development returns, leaving a telltale ring where the interruption occurred. Judging from the area affected on the tooth, Dr. Finnegan concluded its owner probably suffered an extended illness around age five.

Information about the owner's height and race couldn't be arrived at from the bones available, but analysis of the color and structure of the hair samples strongly suggested the person was white.

Analysis also showed it had been a long time since the person died. Dr. Finnegan could tell by examining a cross section of the big-toe bone under an ultraviolet light.

Ultraviolet light excites and activates protein residue in a bone so that the more protein present, the more fluorescent light appears. If fluorescent light appears across the whole bone, the specimen is usually less than one hundred years old. If it shows up only in some areas, it's probably more than one hundred years old.

Dr. Finnegan estimated the big-toe sample to be about a hundred years old, because fluorescent light appeared across most of the bone.

"You've just identified Jesse James," officials told Dr. Finnegan after receiving his forensic report.

"Of course I had not positively identified Jesse James," he says. "However, many of the findings of the osteological report are compatible with what we know about Jesse James from the historical record."

Indeed.

Jesse James was a white man who died at age thirty-five in 1882 — ninety-six years before the bones were retrieved. He also suffered a serious illness at age six, which may have damaged his tooth.

More Forensic Detectives ...
and the Clues They Collect

Computer Specialists

Not all criminals commit crimes with knives and guns. Some log on to trouble using computers. An estimated one trillion dollars is transferred electronically over computers each week, increasing the potential for crime. To stop computer crimes, the FBI has put together a Computer Analysis and Response Team (CART). The team investigates cases involving bank theft, drug dealing, mail fraud, and gambling. In many of these cases, computers are used not only to steal money but also to store illegal business records, which can later be used as evidence. Murderers sometimes even keep computer-based diaries of their crimes. In 1993 CART successfully retrieved plans and maps connected with an attempted murder and cracked one of the largest insurance fraud cases in the United States.

Forensic Pathologists

When police locate a dead body, pathologists examine it, inside and out. They determine the cause and manner of death. Did the victim commit suicide? Did someone else kill him or her? Could it have been an accident? To find out, forensic pathologists investigate the scene where a person died to determine what the victim was doing and his or her health status before death. Next they comb for clues on the victim's clothes, body, and internal organs. The internal exam is called an autopsy. Hairs, threads, and fingernail scrapings are sent to the crime lab for analysis, while blood and urine samples are tested by toxicologists for the presence of alcohol and drugs. Sometimes pathologists determine that victims did not die where they were found, but were moved after death. This, and other information forensic pathologists collect, is valuable to police and can help lead to a killer.

Document Examiners

Whether it's a forged signature on a check or a ransom note written by a kidnapper, document examiners analyze and compare handwriting to determine the author's identity. They also use microscopes to examine hand printing, typewriting, rubber stamps, photocopies, embossed seals, charred documents, and more. When a suspect pen is available, examiners can chemically analyze and compare its ink to that used in a questioned document. Watermarks, translucent impressions that can be seen when paper is held up to light, also provide clues to the true age of a document and the manufacturer. One famous case cracked by document examiners involved a will said to be written by millionaire Howard Hughes. Analysis of the document, which was laced with misspellings and factual errors, revealed the handwriting to be nothing more than a good imitation.

Forensic Toxicologists/Chemists

Sometimes criminals poison their victims. Other times victims poison themselves with overdoses of drugs such as cocaine. To determine whether drugs and alcohol are involved in a crime, forensic toxicologists analyze a victim's blood, urine, and stomach contents. Traces of some drugs also can be found in a victim's hair and bones. Along with studying specimens, these forensic experts assist in arson investigations, where they identify substances used to accelerate fires. They also analyze explosives used in bombings by terrorists and establish the presence of drugs on items such as clothing, cars, and boats.

To identify drugs and explosives at a crime scene, the FBI has developed portable drug detectors called Ionscans. In one case, the equipment helped locate cocaine hidden in railroad ties. In another, it was used to find drugs concealed in dog cages.

Hair and Fiber Examiners

Strands of hair and pieces of fiber can be important clues in a crime-scene investigation. When found, they can help identify the scene of a crime, place suspects at the scene, pinpoint the weapon or the instrument of the crime, or identify hit-and-run vehicles. Although an examination of hair cannot absolutely identify a suspect or victim, it can indicate whether the hair could belong to a particular person. Microscopic analysis of hair can also reveal clues to a person's race, tell which part of the body it came from, and disclose whether it was bleached or burned. Stray fibers help solve crimes, too, by providing circumstantial evidence. Wayne Williams, a serial killer in Atlanta, Georgia, was ar-

rested and eventually convicted after police matched unusual yellow-green carpet fibers found on victims to those in his bedroom.

Firearm Examiners

When guns and bullets are recovered from the scene of a crime, firearms experts take action. They microscopically examine and compare bullets, cartridge cases, and other ammunition components to see if they have been fired from a particular weapon. These forensic examiners also can tell whether a firearm has been discharged and determine the distance at which it was shot by analyzing gunpowder stains on the victim's clothing and the weapon.

To make comparisons more efficient, the FBI recently introduced an automated firearms evidence imaging system called DRUGFIRE. This system stores firearms evidence information and images in a computer database so that police can readily collect, share, and link the evidence to solve crimes. In Baltimore, two murders and another serious shooting were linked by DRUGFIRE over several weeks. Police eventually identified a suspect and recovered the firearm used in all three incidents.

Forensic Science Terms

AFIS (Automated Fingerprint Identification System):
a high-speed computer system that stores fingerprint images and can compare those found at a crime scene with the millions it has on file (p. 19)

anthropologist:
a professional who studies the origins and development of human beings and their cultures (p. 7)

autopsy:
an examination of the internal organs of a corpse to determine cause and manner of death. (p. 44)

cartilage:
the rubbery substance that cushions the bones between joints and makes up the soft portion of the nose and outer ear (p. 20)

criminalist:
a forensic scientist who analyzes, compares, and interprets physical evidence that may link a suspect and victim to a crime. Materials criminalists work with include hair, blood, fibers, firearms, and paint chips.

DNA (deoxyribonucleic acid):
the chemical blueprint that makes us who we are and provides police with a genetic clue to a criminal's identity. DNA can be extracted from cells in blood, skin, saliva, tooth pulp, and other human tissue. (p. 25)

facial reconstruction:
the rebuilding of a person's face by layering clay in various thicknesses over a skull. This technique is used by forensic sculptors to help police identify missing persons. (p. 26)

fingerprint:
the impression left by the tiny ridges on the tips of a person's fingers. Because no two people have the same fingerprints, the impressions are often used in identification (p. 7)

forensic anthropologist:
a physical anthropologist who applies his or her knowledge of the human skeleton to help solve crimes and settle legal matters (p. 7)

forensic dentist:
a dentist who identifies the dead by examining teeth and comparing the information to dental charts. Bite-mark analysis is also part of a forensic dentist's specialty. (p. 7)

forensic entomologist:
a scientist who studies insects and uses the predictable patterns of bug behavior and development to help police solve crimes (p. 30)

forensic pathologist:
a medical scientist who studies diseases and injuries and uses this information to determine cause and manner of death (p. 7)

forensic science:
the study and practice of applying science to solve crimes and settle legal matters (p. 7)

forensic sculptor:
an artist who aids in identifying skeletal remains by reconstructing the face of an

unidentified person using his or her skull as a guide (p. 26)

forensic serologist:
a criminalist who analyzes blood and body fluids (p. 7)

osteology:
the study of bones

osteometric (or bone) board:
a tool for measuring long bones such as those of the thigh and upper arms. These bones are used to estimate a person's height. (p. 21)

physical anthropology:
the study of the changes in the human skeleton as it has evolved over time (p. 7)

sinus print:
the scalloplike pattern on the upper edges of the sinuses, which can be seen in X rays of the forehead. Each person's sinus print is unique and can be used as a means of identification. (p. 24)

skeleton:
the bony framework of the body, which gives people shape and protects their vital organs, including the heart and lungs (p. 7)

skull:
the bony frame of the head, which protects the brain and consists of twenty-nine different bones (p. 7)

superimposition:
used by forensic anthropologists to refer to the overlaying of a skull image with that of a photograph to help verify a person's identity (p. 31)

Bone Biography

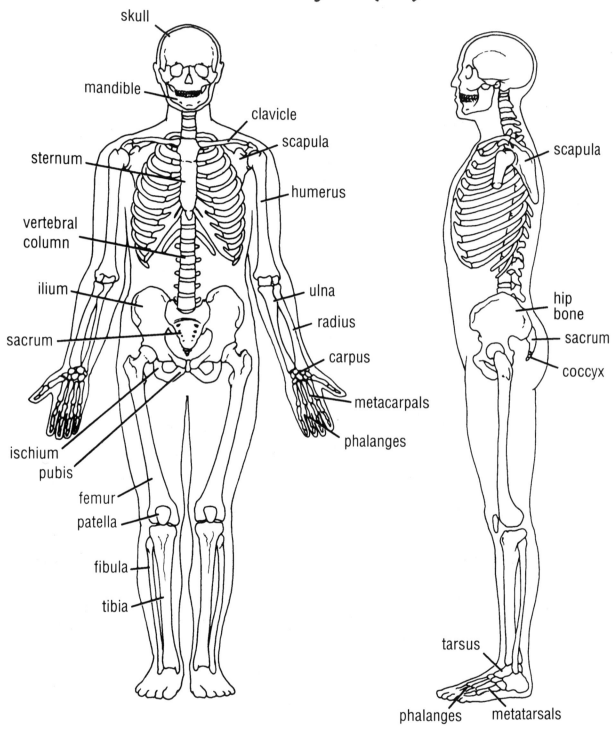

skull

mandible

clavicle

scapula

sternum

humerus

vertebral column

ulna

ilium

radius

sacrum

carpus

metacarpals

phalanges

ischium

pubis

femur

patella

fibula

tibia

scapula

hip bone

sacrum

coccyx

tarsus

phalanges

metatarsals

The adult human skeleton consists of more than two hundred bones, and each contains clues to a person's identity.